AN
EGRET'S
DAY

AN
EGRET'S
DAY

Poems by
JANE YOLEN

Photographs by
JASON STEMPLE

WORDSONG

HONESDALE, PENNSYLVANIA

To Joanne and the twins,
who see egrets every day
—J.Y.

For Carol Case, Karen Bacot,
and my mom, the three ladies
who helped me turn a passion
into a career
—J.S.

Eight Words About an Egret

Grass stalks,
Then grass walks.
Look out, fish.

Egret Greets the Sun: A Haiku

Egret on a dock.
How will he rinse out morning
Stains from his feathers?

The Great Egret's Name

*Different countries have different names for this bird.
In France it is called* Grande Aigrette. Garza blanca
or Garza grande *is its name in Spain. The Latin name
is* Ardea alba. *In English it's also known as the Common
Egret, American Egret, and—in old-world literature—
as the Great White Heron.*

Contents

Where Do Egrets Walk?

One of the most widespread of the egrets, the Great Egret is an elegant wading bird of the heron family. It often walks in the shallows of lakes, freshwater and saltwater marshes, ponds, rice fields, mudflats, and seashores. It also strides through swampy woods, tidal estuaries, lagoons, mangroves, and along streams. The tracks of a Great Egret are huge compared with those of many other waders.

Great Egret

The Great Egret's wings
are like fresh sheets
hung out upon a line;
its neck is a telescope;
beak as sharp and fine
as a fisherman's gutting knife;
legs thin dark stalks,
sprung wires, steel skewers.
I watch as it walks
through the mud and water,
through the swamp and more—
all along the humpy, bumpy,
     shallow, sandy shore.

What Do Egrets Eat?

Great Egrets are known as "ambush predators," waiting silently for the prey to come to them. They are very good at the waiting game. Great Egrets eat crayfish, frogs, algae, and—most of all—fish. But they also devour occasional snakes, anoles, and even small birds, as well as many insects. When they spot something to eat, egrets pull their heads and necks backward, then stab forward quickly at the prey.

10

On the Hunt

He is a world-class waiter,
Waiting (and wading)
In the muddied water
Till a shadow below
Lets him know that a fish
Is near. Then *SPLISH-*
SPLASH, that knife-sharp beak
Breaks the surface
And brings back a surfeit:
Breakfast, lunch, dinner.
Almost every strike a winner.

Egret in Flight

She's an arrow
From a bow.
We watch in wonder
From below.

Origami
Neck is folded.
All that we can do?
Behold it.

Angel wings
Of purest white.
Perfect flyer.
Perfect flight.

How to Fly Egret-Style

Notice how the Great Egret folds up its long neck in flight, a kind of peculiar bird origami. The long black legs, extended full length, act as a rudder. The wings, five feet from one tip to the other, seem full of light.

What Is Preening?

*Egrets spend a lot of time preening—
smoothing or cleaning feathers with
their beak or bill. The bird removes
parasites and keeps the feathers
water resistant by taking materials
from its oil gland and powder-down
patches and applying them to the
feathers. Feathers are important to a
bird's life both on the water and on
the wing. So they must be inspected,
cleaned, corrected—preened—many
times a day.*

Preening Egret

He is his own Laundromat,
And when he does his preening
He polishes the place he sat—
His beak so good for cleaning.

He mucks between each feather,
He plucks and primps and pries.
In every kind of weather
He washes and he dries.

How dirty can a bird get
That lives on sand, sea, air?
The talented Great Egret
Is truly wash-and-wear.

Plumes

Its plumes resemble Belgian lace
That ladies wear most any place.
However, plumes like these should stay—
No matter what hat makers pay—
Upon the shoulders of the egret.
My take on this is hardly secret.

The Use and Abuse of Egret Feathers

Egret feathers—also called plumes—are beautiful and frosty white, especially during breeding season. Up close, they truly look like lace. At one time the plumes were much sought after for decorating clothing and hats. In the late nineteenth and early part of the twentieth century, an ounce of egret plumes was worth an ounce of gold.

Head and Beak

The Great Egret's long neck is often S-shaped when standing or flying. His beak is easy to identify as it is long and yellow. Watch out, though. The beak is the Great Egret's weapon. With it he spears his meals.

Close-up

As conscious of his beauty
As any Hollywood star,
The egret poses.

He supposes
Your camera is not very far
And that you will do your duty.

Click. Click.
The egret's composure is not shaken
Even when his close-up's taken.

Some Feet

Some feet may look quite pretty
Upon a tiny bird.
Some feet may look quite silly,
And some feet quite absurd.

The Great's splayed feet walk easily
In water and on land,
Yet strong enough for clinging,
As mobile as a hand.

Great Egret

Distinguishing Egret Feet

Look at those feet! Size is not the only characteristic that distinguishes the Great Egret from the Snowy Egret. Great Egrets have black feet, and Snowy Egrets have yellow feet, often called "golden slippers." Although Great Egrets find their food mostly by standing and waiting, occasionally they also use their large feet with the long toes to rake and probe the bottom of the water. This foraging method dislodges crayfish and attracts fish, making Great Egrets among the best fishermen in the animal kingdom.

Snowy Egret

Reflection

How easy to fall in love
With one's own reflection.
If only the egret's simple perfection,
Below and above,

Were clearly female/male.
But where egrets are concerned
Gender's a hard lesson to be learned,
And many birders fail.

Is It a Male or a Female?

*It is hard to tell apart the sexes of the Great Egret
without actually capturing them. But anyone trying
to catch a Great Egret to check its gender had better
be prepared. The bird makes a deep croaking sound
when disturbed, and remember that sharp beak!*

How Big Are Great Egrets?

*The Great Egret stands between 37 and 41 inches tall.
(That's 94 to 104 centimeters.) A full-grown adult egret's
wingspan is 52 to 58 inches wide (in centimeters, 131 to 145).
That's about a 5-foot spread, the size of a small human.*

Measure Me

I am a tower
of strength,
a bird
of great length.
I am tall,
of much height,
a long arrow
in flight.
My wings
almost span
the full length
of a man.

Look on me
and delight
if you will,
if you can.

Nesting:
An Egret Limerick

Our home—it is here in the sticks,
With three very boisterous chicks.
They bully and fight
Until they take flight,
But it's nothing that we cannot fix.

What Does an Egret Nest Look Like?

The nest of a Great Egret is made up of sticks and reeds and is often high up in a tree, although in coastal regions they may nest in scrub near the ground. The female can lay as many as six eggs, but a usual clutch is three. Not all the hatchlings survive, and the larger chicks often kill the smaller ones. However, aggressive siblings are not the only danger. Great Egrets are vulnerable as well to egg-stealing raccoons and to Great Horned Owls, which carry off the chicks.

27

An Egret's Roost

Great Egrets hunt by day, and at night they roost in trees or swamp bushes, most often with other egrets and herons in communal colonies. They usually head toward their roosts about an hour before sunset. Sometimes hundreds of birds roost in the same tree.

The Egret Goes Home to Her Roost

Bedtime—and like an arrow loosed,
The Great Egret flies back to roost
With others of her company
To decorate a greening tree.

Like great white balls, they seem to light
The soft and mellow southern night.
They sleep the dusky dark away,
To rise again and greet the day.

I Saw a Great Egret Today

I saw a Great Egret today
Standing on a wooden dock.
Humans and egrets, we are just
A tick of evolution's clock.

I wondered as we stood so still,
If in a hundred years or more,
Would egrets still fly through the skies?
Would humans still watch from the shore?

Humans Versus Egrets

The history between humans and egrets has not always been a happy one. The birds' glorious feathers, long used for human adornment, meant that certain egret populations were all but wiped out by the early twentieth century. Although egret numbers have been restored, wetlands polluted with chemicals or pesticides still put egrets at great risk. In some ways, the Great Egret populations are a good reminder of how far we have come in protecting this beautiful species—and how far we still have to go.

The publisher thanks Dr. John H. Rappole,
an ornithologist and scientist emeritus at the
Smithsonian National Zoological Park, for
reviewing the poetry. Dr. Rappole is also
chairman of the board of trustees of the
Roger Tory Peterson Institute.

Wordsong
An Imprint of Boyds Mills Press, Inc.
815 Church Street
Honesdale, Pennsylvania 18431
Printed in the United States of America

Library of Congress Cataloging-in-Publication Data

Yolen, Jane.
  An egret's day / poems by Jane Yolen ; photographs
by Jason Stemple. — 1st ed.
    p. cm.
  ISBN 978-1-59078-650-5 (alk. paper)
1. Herons—Juvenile poetry. 2. Herons—Juvenile
literature. 3. Children's poetry, American.
I. Stemple, Jason, ill. II. Title.

  PS3575.O43E47 2009
  811'.54—dc22

2008051688

First edition
The text of this book is set in 14-point Wilke Roman.

10 9 8 7 6 5 4 3 2 1